Prayers of the Heart

KARYN MICHONSKI

PRAYERS OF THE HEART

My thanks...

To the one and only living God the Father, God the Son, and God the Holy Spirit, for impressing upon my heart these prayers in response to the influences in and on my life, and for making them part of my daily prayers.

Two of these influences need to be mentioned: the *Jesus Calling* books by Sarah Young (which have been a part of my daily devotions for years); and Chris Tomlin, an exceptional singer and songwriter whose music, books, devotionals, and interviews have been pure blessings.

Thanks also to the Daughters of the Holy Cross; becoming a member led to my

writing down all these prayers
in a journal.

Thanks as well to my mom,
whose approving response to a
few of these prayers planted
within me the idea of writing
them all down for God to use
as he pleases.

And finally, my thanks to
our son Timmy for using his
talents as an artist and graphic
designer to make the cover and
illustrations.

Soli Deo Gloria.

*I dedicate this book
to our son Justin,
the oldest of the triplets.
May God continue to guide you
in your discernment
and in everything you do.*

Dear reader,

It is my hope that some of these prayers will speak to your heart, that you will find them easy to use, and that they will help you deepen your relationship with God.

—Karyn

Prayers
of the
Heart

It seems I am here again, dear God, with nowhere else to turn. I must put my trust in you, a lesson I hope to learn.

Dear God, please send me an angel; I sure could use the help. It's good to know that when times are troubled, I'm not all by myself.

 Show me what to do, dear God, and help me follow through, for I know that I can put my hope and trust in you.

In Jesus's name, Amen.

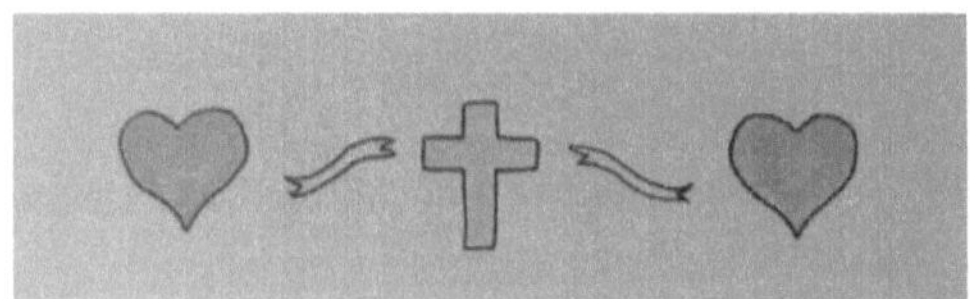

Lord Jesus, thank you for everything.

Please forgive my sins, and remove them from me as far as the east is from the west.[1]

Lord Jesus, I consecrate my thoughts, words, intentions, actions, reactions, dreams, desires, feelings, fantasies, deeds, and heart to you. Please purify them for you.

Holy Spirit, please quiet my mind, my spirit, and my heart so I can hear God's voice and think God's thoughts.

Holy Spirit, please help me to
tell the difference between
God's voice and the devil's.
Help me to turn away from the
devil right away every time.

Holy Spirit, please control
completely my mind, my
thoughts, my words, my
intentions, my actions, my
reactions, my dreams, my
desires, my feelings, my
fantasies, my deeds, and my
heart.

Holy Spirit, please think
through me, pray through me,
talk through me, listen through
me, live through me, and love
through me.

Holy Spirit, please protect me
from everything and anything
that the devil can snare me
with. And please bounce out of
me permanently all of his
snares, no matter how deep
they go.

Please especially bounce out of
me anything and everything
that can interfere with my
relationship with Jesus.

Holy Spirit, please bounce out
of me permanently all doubts
and fears, except for the fear of
God.

Holy Spirit, please bounce out
of me permanently all regrets
and resentments from the past.

Holy Spirit, please continuously purify my thoughts, words, intentions, actions, reactions, dreams, desires, feelings, fantasies, and heart.

Lord Jesus, please be a part of my thoughts, feelings, and decisions today and always.[2]

Holy Spirit, please fill me with God's love, peace, and joy.

Holy Spirit, please empower my prayers, and help me pray more effectively, efficiently, and abundantly with a clearer mind and a thankful heart.

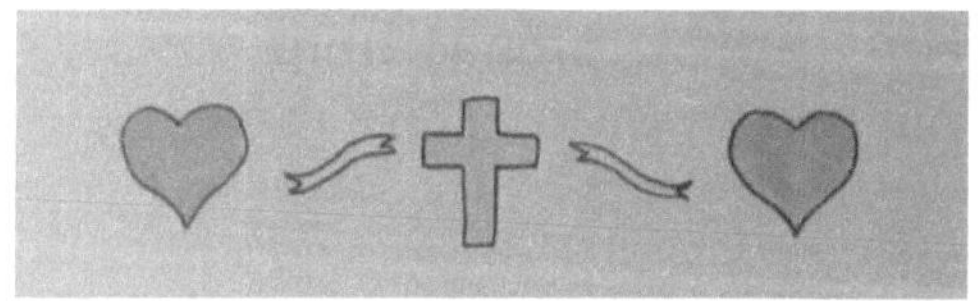

Holy Spirit, please help me
make Jesus my default focus.[2]

Please help me make a
permanent place in my mind
for God, where I will notice him
always.

Holy Spirit, please help me to
always be aware of God's
presence, no matter what I am
doing.

Please help me lean on God
completely and continuously.

Holy Spirit, please help me persevere in keeping my eyes on Jesus.[2]

Holy Spirit, please help me when my mind wanders, slips into neutral, or flies off into fantasyland. Help me instead to think of God in the present.

Please alert me when I'm paying too much attention to this world and its problems, and turn my attention back to God.

Please prevent and protect me from making anything an idol, and help me to worship only God.

Please alert me when I'm trying
to control something, and help
me to submit my will to God's.

Please alert me when the devil
is trying to deceive me, and
help me turn to Jesus right
away for help every time.

Holy Spirit, please take control
of the details of this day, and
line them up according to
God's will for me.

Lord Jesus, please orchestrate
the events of my day today,
and show me what to do.

Holy Spirit, please open my
eyes to receive God's gifts.

Please open my heart to receive
God's gifts, presence, love, and
guidance in every way that he
sends them to me.

Holy Spirit, please guide me
every step of the way down the
path of life that God has
chosen for me.

Lord Jesus, thank you, thank
you, thank you for choosing
this path of life for me.

Holy Spirit, please help me to
perceive, receive, and accept
with thankfulness and
humbleness all the blessings
God gives me.

Please help me to always instantly, unconditionally, and humbly accept the grace God gives me, and the love and mercy he gives me.

Please help me to look at my life through the lens of gratitude.

Holy Spirit, please fill me with the fullness of God.

Please help me get to know God's love fully, to fully receive and experience and accept it, and to have it shine from my face continuously. Help me understand it so I can share this love with others.

Holy Spirit, please grant me
courage to share God's love
with others.

Holy Spirit, please help me
understand your Scripture and
my faith the way God intends
me to understand them.

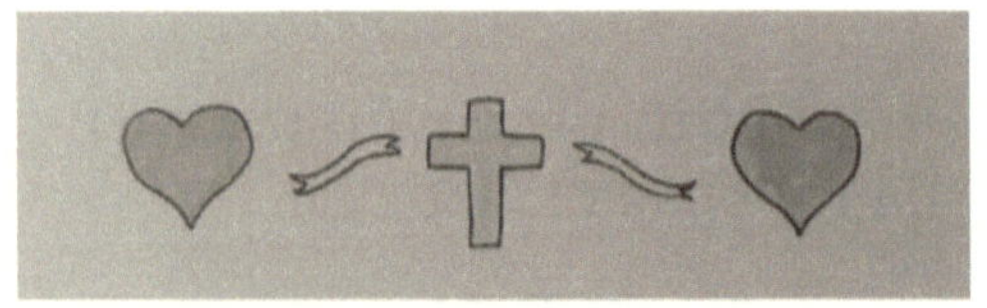

Holy Spirit, thank you for all
the prayers you pray for me.
Thank you for all the help you
give me.

Thank you for loving me. I
stand in awe of you. I adore
you, Holy Spirit.

Lord Jesus, thank you, thank
you, thank you for the gift of
the Holy Spirit.

Holy Spirit and Lord Jesus,
please keep me aware of your
presence every moment of my
life.

Holy Spirit and Lord Jesus,
please make me more receptive
to your presence, and help me
notice you more fully, more
clearly, more distinctly and
continuously.

Lord Jesus, please prepare me
fully for everything you have
planned for me.

Lord Jesus, please increase my thankfulness. Train me to trust you more consistently, and help me treasure your joy in my heart and share it with others.

Lord Jesus, thank you for drawing me near to you and awakening my heart to you.

Thank you for blessing me with your love, joy, and peace.

Lord Jesus, I open myself up completely to you. I give my life to you.

Please show me what to do, and help me do it.

Cleanse me from my sinfulness. Purify my thoughts and the desires of my heart completely, continuously, and permanently. And love me, I pray. Thank you!

Lord Jesus, thank you for this day. Thank you for every breath I take. Thank you for every beat of my heart.

Thank you for my ability to see, hear, move, think, talk, act, and feel.

Thank you for your patience, protection, and guidance.

Thank you for your forgiveness and mercy.

Thank you for your love for me and for your sacrifice on the cross.

I stand in awe of you, Lord Jesus! I adore you.

I love and adore you, heavenly Father! Thank you for the gift of Jesus.

Thank you for choosing me to be your beloved child.

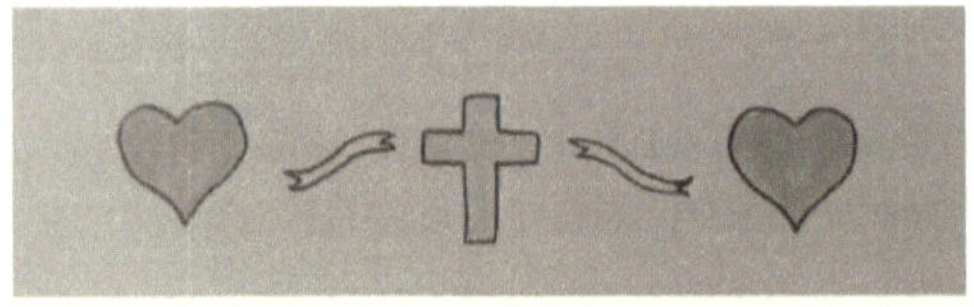

Please cleanse me from all unrighteous judgment toward other people. And help me never again to judge others in this way.

Lord Jesus, please help me in everything.

My life belongs to you, Lord Jesus. Please help me become the person you designed and created me to be, the person you want me to be.

Please help me do what you want me to do.

Lord Jesus, please help me to
distinctly feel your love and
presence, and the love and
presence of God the Father and
God the Holy Spirit. Help me
do this all day today, and all
night tonight.

Lord Jesus, please glorify your
name through me.

Lord Jesus, make me strong in
my work for you, and help me
to give the credit to you alone.

In all my activities, please help
me search for you and find
you.

Lord Jesus, please help me love
you the way you created me to
love you.

Please make my love for you
strong enough and deep
enough that it can never be
affected in a negative way.

Lord Jesus, please make my
love grow stronger for you, for
God the Father, and for God
the Holy Spirit. Deepen this
love far beyond measure
throughout the rest of my days
on earth and throughout all
eternity.

Lord Jesus, I want to learn all
about you.

Lord Jesus, please help me to
forgive myself and others.

Please help me to empty myself completely of me and to live only for you.

Lord Jesus, please increase my confidence in you, and drive away all doubt forever.

Holy Spirit, help me be honest and open with God.[2]

Lord Jesus, thy will be done in my life. Please show me where and how you want me to serve you.

Holy Spirit, free me from all self-centeredness.

Holy Spirit, help me look beyond myself with eyes that really see.[2]

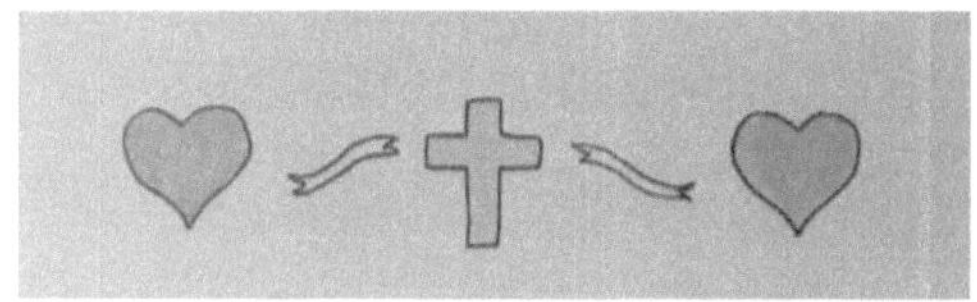

Lord Jesus, please reveal your nature to me, and help me to be that way too, especially in humbleness.

Lord Jesus, please develop in me a confidence to trust you anytime you have an assignment for me.[10]

Lord Jesus, please reveal to me the true nature of my relationship with you. And please bring me into a genuine intimacy with you and with the Holy Spirit, an intimacy that is strong, deep, and permanent.

Holy Spirit, please help me love God with all my being.

Lord Jesus, for the rest of my life, please grant me a tender and sensitive heart that responds "yes" to your will at the slightest prompting by your Spirit.

Lord Jesus, help me always to be able to recognize your voice above all others, and to do so right away.

Holy Spirit, please guide my
prayers so they are according
to God's will and only God's
will.[10]

Lord Jesus, please increase my
faith to believe you in all
things. Help me walk by faith
no matter what the outcome.[10]

Search my heart, Lord Jesus,
and help me get rid of anything
in it that is displeasing to you.

Holy Spirit, help me become
comfortable talking about God
with people I meet.

Lord Jesus, please take me into
a deeper knowledge and
experience of your love and
tenderness.

Holy Spirit, empower and guide me in the adventure of knowing God's love.

Holy Spirit, please help me deal with difficulties as needed, and help me reserve the bulk of my attention for Jesus.[2]

Holy Spirit, please protect my mind and my heart from distractions, distortions, deception, anxiety, and other entanglements, so without hindrance I can search for and find God in my daily activities.[2]

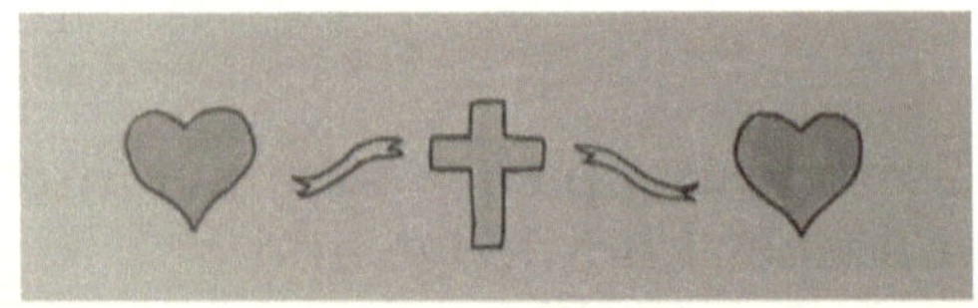

Lord Jesus, guide me into
hopes and dreams that are in
line with your will. Thy will be
done fully in my life, and only
thy will be done in my life.
Infuse your desires into my
heart, Lord Jesus.

Holy Spirit, help me to accept
the hopes and dreams and the
love of family and friends that
God leads me to.

Lord Jesus, open my eyes and
my heart to discern all your
communications to me.[2]

Lord, lead me into the depths
of your life, and save me from a
shallow existence.[4]

Holy Spirit and Lord Jesus,
help me stop comparing myself
and my life to that of other
people, and help me to never
do this again.

Please help me take captive
every thought and make it
obedient to you, Lord Jesus.[3]

Lord Jesus, please cleanse me
from all my strongholds
permanently.[5]

Lord Jesus, help me to choose
to be joyful at all times.

Lord Jesus, please help me to
look at my past and my life
from your perspective.

Lord Jesus, help me accept
and be content with the life you
have given me.

Holy Spirit, help me receive
and accept God's love in
greater depth, breadth, and
constancy everyday.

Holy Spirit, help me meditate
on God's loving presence, and
bring my mind back to God
whenever it wanders.[2]

Holy Spirit, please help me to
keep God as my first love.[5a]

Holy Spirit, please help me to
open myself fully—heart, mind,
and spirit—to God's living
presence.

Lord Jesus, help me overcome
my unbelief.[9]

Holy Spirit, please quiet my
spirit so I can hear God's voice
in every situation I encounter.

Lord Jesus, I open my arms
and my heart to receive your
delight in me in full measure.

Holy Spirit, help me remember
that God is always with me.[5b]

Fill me to overflowing with your
presence, Lord Jesus.

Holy Spirit, help me to never
balk at receiving a gift from
God.

Holy Spirit, help me obey God every time he tells me to do something, and to obey right away and with a thankful attitude.

Holy Spirit, help me get rid of anything that is preventing me from obeying Jesus.

Holy Spirit, help me to always recognize God's communications to me.

Holy Spirit, help me make the connections God wants me to make between my prayers and the events in my life.

Lord Jesus, I want you to be central in all my thoughts, feelings, plans, and actions.[2]

Lord Jesus, fill me to
overflowing with the Holy Spirit
so He flows through me
constantly, and is always seen
by others in me.

Holy Spirit, help me see God
more clearly.[6]

Holy Spirit, please
communicate the deep things
of God to my spirit.[6]

Help me to not be gullible or
deceived by people, but to
prayerfully follow your lead,
Lord Jesus, in everything.

Holy Spirit, purify me from my
sin, and reveal Christ Jesus in
me.

Lord Jesus, please be yourself
in me.

Holy Spirit, teach me, lead me,
and work through me for your
glory.[6]

Lord Jesus, make me obedient
and sensitive to your Spirit at
all times.

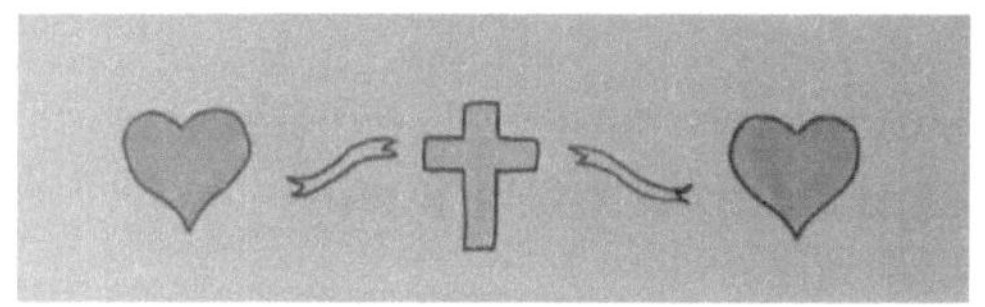

Holy Spirit, help me to notice
and follow through with all of
the opportunities God provides
to be a blessing to others.

Create in me a clean heart, O God, and renew a right spirit within me.[7]

Lord Jesus, forgive me, cleanse me, and use me as you will.[6]

Lord Jesus, please show me the purpose you have for my life, and help me fulfill it with you.

Purify my heart, Lord Jesus, and keep it pure for all eternity.

Holy Spirit, help me to always pray all my prayers with the faith of God.

Holy Spirit, keep my eyes and my mind wide open to all that God is doing in my life.

Holy Spirit, I give you the entire responsibility of closing every road and stopping every step in my life that is not of God. Let me hear and obey your voice when I turn the wrong way.[4]

Lord Jesus, I long for you; please come back soon!

Lord Jesus, prevent me from being negative about anything, and prevent the negativity and fears that I bump up against in my daily life from bringing me down and turning me away from trusting you.

Lord Jesus, help me obtain and keep a quiet and gentle spirit.

Lord Jesus, permeate all my moments with your presence.[2]

Holy Spirit, please help me train my mind to be aware of God even when other things are demanding my attention.[2]

Lord Jesus, clear out the confusion in my mind so I can communicate deeply with you.

Holy Spirit, help me wait patiently and humbly for God to answer my prayers.

Lord Jesus, thank you for allowing me to be here and for giving me the opportunity to do your work with you.

Lord Jesus, open my eyes so I can see everything you have prepared for me today.[2]

Lord Jesus, help me to see beyond the obvious and to find the treasures hidden in my troubles.[2]

Holy Spirit, fill me with contagious delight.[2]

Holy Spirit, help me pause before responding to people or situations, so that I allow you to grace my thoughts, words, and behaviors.[2]

Holy Spirit, guide me moment
by moment throughout this
day.

Lord Jesus, please prevent me
from letting my past taint my
view of the future.

Lord Jesus, establish your
work in my life to a depth that
nothing can rob me of the joy
that comes from knowing that I
belong to you.[9]

Holy Spirit, cleanse and free
me from everything that is
preventing me from drawing
closer to God.[9]

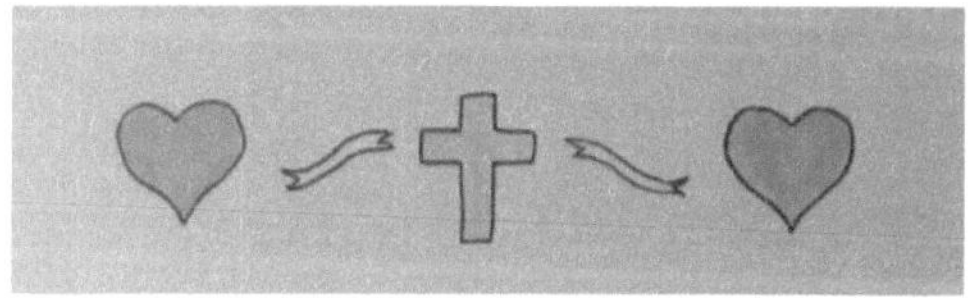

I have faith in God that it will happen just as he told me.[8]

I am fully known, fully forgiven, and forever loved and accepted by Jesus.

I pray all my prayers in your name Lord Jesus.

Notes...

[1]Psalm 103:12 (KJV)

[2]From the books by Sarah Young, *Jesus Calling* (Nashville, Thomas Nelson, 2004), *Jesus Today* (2012), *Jesus Always* (2016).

[3]2 Cor 10:5 (KJV)

[4]From *Streams in the Desert* by L.B. Cowman, (Grand Rapids, Zondervan, 1992)

[5]Inspired by Chris Tomlin's songs, *Strongholds*, (Always, 2022); [a]*First Love*,(Never Lose Sight, 2016); [b]*Whom Shall I Fear (Angel Armies)*, (Burning Lights, 2013).

[6]From *Experiencing the Spirit* by Henry and Melvin Blackaby, (New York, Multnomah, 2009)

[7]Psalm 51:10 (KJV)

[8] Acts 27:25 (KJV)

[9]From *Unlimiting God* by Richard Blackaby, (New York, Multnomah, 2008)

[10]From *Experiencing God* by Henry and Richard Blackaby, Claude V. King, (Nashville, B&H, 2008)

*Some of the prayers that are not marked are the result of the influences of Chris Tomlin's songs and interviews, Sarah Young's books, Richard Blackaby's books, and *Streams in the Desert* by L.B. Cowman.

Acknowledgements...

Thank you to God for guiding me through the process of creating this book.

Thanks to Thomas Womack (Book Ox) for editing this project.